What Is the Story of Scooby-Doo?

What Is the Story of Scooby-Doo?

by M. D. Payne

illustrated by Andrew Thomson

Penguin Workshop

For E. R. Bullis, lover of spooky mysteries—MDP

For Rhia and all "Those Meddling Kids"—AT

PENGUIN WORKSHOP
An Imprint of Penguin Random House LLC, New York

WEB CODE: PEUS40095

Published by Penguin Workshop, an imprint of Penguin Random House LLC, New York.
PENGUIN and PENGUIN WORKSHOP are trademarks of Penguin Books Ltd.
WHO HQ & Design is a registered trademark of Penguin Random House LLC.
Printed in the USA.

Visit us online at www.penguinrandomhouse.com.

Library of Congress Cataloging-in-Publication Data is available upon request.

ISBN 9781524788247 (paperback)   10 9 8
ISBN 9781524788254 (library binding)   10 9 8 7 6 5 4 3 2 1

Contents

What Is the Story of Scooby-Doo? 1

A Star Is Born 4

Quite the Character 14

Scooby-Who? 20

Mystery Inc. 34

Scooby-Doo Takes Over TV 42

Puppy Power! 54

Scooby Beyond Television 66

Scooby Takes Over TV . . . Again! 80

The Legacy of Scooby-Doo 91

What's Next for Scooby-Doo? 102

Bibliography 106

What Is the Story of Scooby-Doo?

On the morning of September 13, 1969, children all around the United States were watching Saturday morning cartoons on TV. But this morning was special. This morning, the first episode of the cartoon *Scooby-Doo, Where Are You!* was shown on the CBS network.

The name of the episode was "What a Night for a Knight." It featured a group of four teenagers—Fred, Daphne, Velma, and Shaggy—and a big goofy dog, Scooby-Doo. They followed clues to solve a spooky mystery. A knight's armor was shipped from England to America for display in a museum. But the professor who sent the armor to the museum had disappeared—and the armor of the Black Knight was alive! The kids and their talking dog, Scooby-Doo, needed to avoid the

Black Knight while figuring out what happened to the professor.

By the end of the episode, the teens had solved the mystery—and children around the country had fallen in love with the Great Dane named Scooby-Doo. The show quickly became one of

the most popular cartoons ever. Children and adults tuned in for the mysteries. They sang the theme song. They liked the silly villains. Mostly, they loved the star of the show, Scooby-Doo.

Was Scooby a superhero? Certainly not! He was a scaredy-cat . . . well, a scaredy-dog! But he would always help his friends solve the mystery, no matter how spooky, in exchange for a Scooby Snack. This dog, who didn't even realize how brave he was, stumbled into hundreds of mysteries, and into the hearts of viewers around the world. But Scooby is more than just a talking dog. He has conquered television, comics, movies, books, and more—in more than 160 countries.

Scooby-Doo is one of the most famous dogs of all time, and this is his story.

CHAPTER 1
A Star Is Born

The original idea for *Scooby-Doo, Where Are You!* was much different from what viewers saw on that first Saturday morning in 1969. Cartoons were developed by teams of talented and creative people. As a new show was developed, there were many opinions about how it should look.

Fred Silverman came up with the original idea for Scooby-Doo in 1968. Fred was the head of daytime programming for CBS, a major television network. Fred wanted a show with teenagers and music and mystery. But Fred just had the idea—he didn't know how to make the cartoon!

Fred Silverman

At the time, cartoons were very popular on Saturday morning television. Children around the country tuned in for their favorites: *The Jetsons*, *Spider-Man*, *Casper the Friendly Ghost*, and many others.

An animation company called Hanna-Barbera Productions made some of the most popular cartoons. In fact, they had made the most popular cartoon of all time up until that point: *The Flintstones*. So, Fred went to the producers William Hanna and Joseph Barbera with his idea, knowing that they might be able to turn it into a smash hit!

Cartoons!

Cartoons began to appear in movie theaters in the United States shortly after movies first became popular, in 1906. Unfortunately, cartoons were very difficult to make. The artists—called animators—had to draw, by hand, twenty-four frames of a cartoon for every *second* of film. That means even a three-minute cartoon would require an animator to draw 4,320 pictures!

In 1914, the "animation cel"—a background that could remain the same—was created. Now, only characters in front of the background had to be changed. This made it much easier to create the twenty-four frames for each second.

By the early 1930s, storyboards—a group of sketches that told the story of the entire cartoon—were drawn before animators started their work. This allowed a team of people to work to create a longer cartoon. Each animator took on a small piece of the cartoon, and longer, more complex stories could be told with cartoon animation.

Hanna-Barbera's team of writers, led by Joe Ruby and Ken Spears, thought up a show called *Mysteries Five* about five teenagers and a shaggy dog named "Too Much." During the day, the teenagers were musicians—Too Much played the bongos. They solved spooky mysteries at night. The stories were filled with ghosts and monsters.

Joe Ruby and Ken Spears

Joe and Ken presented their first idea to Fred. But Fred didn't think it was quite right. He liked the mystery and music, but wasn't sure about the characters. He worked with Joe and Ken to change them. Five teenagers became four—Fred, Daphne, Velma, and Shaggy. The sheepdog became a Great Dane. Fred also changed the title of the show to *Who's S-S-Scared?*

Satisfied with the new show idea, Fred presented it to his bosses at CBS. But they worried that the answer to *Who's S-S-Scared?* would be "little kids"! A parents' group called Action for Children's Television was protesting that television shows for children were too violent and scary—and CBS was listening. They didn't want to produce a show that was too scary for kids. So CBS said no to Fred and *Who's S-S-Scared?*

Action for Children's Television

Action for Children's Television (ACT) was created in 1968 to help improve children's television. It started as a small group of parent volunteers in the homes of two mothers. Led by founder Peggy Charren, it went on to become a massive movement

driven by a large budget, a full-time staff, and twenty thousand volunteers!

One of ACT's first successes was making Saturday morning cartoons less violent. ACT would go on to do many great things for children, including limiting the amount and types of advertising they saw, and making more children's shows available.

ACT's biggest success came with the passing of the Children's Television Act in 1990, which required broadcasters to feature a certain amount of educational programming for children each day. Shortly after the passing of the act, Peggy decided that the organization's work was done, and the organization was closed.

Fred was still determined to make his idea for *Who's S-S-Scared?* a reality. He worked with Joe and Ken at Hanna-Barbera Productions to change the idea once again. They came back with a new idea for Fred. Although the mysteries were still spooky, the monsters were not real. At the end of each story, they would turn out to be just bad guys in disguise.

The rock band idea was dropped, and the characters became much funnier—especially the dog. The goofy Great Dane was now the star.

Fred thought kids would be too busy laughing to be scared.

The executives at CBS agreed, and *Scooby-Doo, Where Are You!* was born!

CHAPTER 2
Quite the Character

The character of Scooby-Doo was the result of many creative people's work—executives, writers, artists, actors, and directors. They all contributed ideas for how Scooby-Doo should look and act, what his name should be, and what he would say. But in the end, there were two people most responsible for bringing Scooby to life.

Iwao Takamoto was the character designer who gave Scooby his look.

A woman that Iwao worked with owned a number of Great Danes—the very large type of dog Scooby is. Iwao asked her what the perfect Great Dane would look like. She told him that the most prized Great Danes have strong chins, straight ears, and strong legs.

Great Dane

But Iwao knew Scooby had to look like a big scaredy-cat— not strong like most Great Danes. So, he drew Scooby with a small chin, droopy ears, and crooked legs—the exact opposite of what a "perfect" Great Dane should look like! Iwao also

gave Scooby a very expressive face, which could go from spooked to brave to silly— depending on his mood.

Iwao Takamoto (1925–2007)

Japanese American illustrator Iwao Takamoto designed more than one thousand cartoon characters.

Iwao (say: ee-wa-oh) grew up during World War II in California. During the war, Japan was fighting against the United States. Because of that, Americans did not trust the Japanese—even those who were legal American citizens. The US government placed Japanese Americans like Iwao in "internment camps." It was in one of these camps that Iwao met two illustrators. They noticed the skills of this young artist and encouraged him to make a career of it.

After the war was over, and Iwao left the camp, he wanted to share his work with animation studios. But Iwao didn't have enough money for a professional portfolio (a collection of his work). So instead, he put together a sketchbook of everything he could draw and presented it to Disney Animation Studios. Disney was so impressed with the young artist's work, they hired him the same day. At Disney, he designed characters and helped illustrate animated films like *Cinderella* and *One Hundred and One Dalmatians.*

In 1961, he started working for Hanna-Barbera Productions, where he went on to design many well-known cartoon characters. His work influenced a number of younger illustrators and designers. He received many honors, including those from the Japanese American National Museum and the Animation Guild.

Voice actor Don Messick gave Scooby his special way of speaking. Don was already known

for voicing many other characters, including other cartoon dogs like Astro from *The Jetsons*. What he created for Scooby-Doo was the voice of a dog who could only talk well enough to be understood by those closest to him.

Don Messick

Don made Scooby sound like a human who had a lot of woofs and barks stuck in his mouth. And it was this unique voice, as much as his look, that made Scooby who he truly was.

And what about his name, that name he howled out at the end of every episode? Before Fred Silverman presented the final idea for his show to CBS, he thought up a new name for the dog. In the late 1960s, one of the most popular songs was "Strangers in the Night" by one of the greatest singers of all time, Frank Sinatra. At the end of the song, Sinatra sings nonsense lyrics: "Dooby dooby doo." Fred listened to the song, and in a

burst of inspiration, changed "Dooby doo" into "Scooby-Doo." Fred thought it was the perfect name for the silly dog.

CHAPTER 3
Scooby-Who?

Scooby-Doo is seven years old. His full name is Scoobert, although only his mother, Momsy-Doo, calls him that. His father's name is Dada-Doo. His grandfather, Grandpa Scooby, lives in Doo Manor—a spooky mansion haunted by Great-Grandpa Scooby.

Scooby comes from a big family. He has three brothers, Howdy-Doo, Skippy-Doo, and Yabba-Doo. Yabba-Doo lives in the southwestern United States and belongs to a deputy (which is something like a sheriff). He also has a sister, Ruby-Doo. Ruby-Doo's son, Scrappy-Doo, occasionally helps his uncle Scooby solve mysteries.

Howdy-Doo

Skippy-Doo

Ruby-Doo

Yabba-Doo

Scrappy-Doo

Scooby has many cousins. Dooby Dooby-Doo is a famous singer. Scooby-Dee is a movie star. Dixie-Doo is Scooby's southern cousin—and is also a singer. Scooby-Dum isn't that smart, but like Scrappy-Doo, sometimes solves mysteries with Scooby-Doo.

Dixie-Doo

Dooby Dooby-Doo

Scooby-Dee

Scooby-Dum

The members of Scooby's family are different than other dogs because they can talk. Scooby doesn't usually talk much—but he says a lot with the few words he knows. He puts an "R" at the front of all of his words. "Ruh-roh" and "relp!" are common words (Scooby-speak for *uh-oh* and *help!*). He also uses his whole body when he talks—waving his paws and pointing. His expressive face helps people to understand him.

Scooby has an all-powerful nose that can sniff out clues and help solve the mysteries. Though his ears are floppy, he has fantastic hearing and is always listening for clues. Scooby's tail is very much like Scooby—most of the time it's scared stiff! But, when necessary, it can transform into a tool that helps Scooby and his friends. It can grab and hold things, pick locks, and even paddle water as fast as a motorboat! Scooby's tail has helped him out of many sticky situations.

Norville "Shaggy" Rogers is Scooby's best friend. But Shaggy does more than take care of Scooby. Together they share a love of food. They're always ready for their next meal—and for tons of snacks between meals. Shaggy is an expert at crafting super-sized sandwiches.

But Shaggy and Scooby are also happy to chow on simple snacks, like the famous "Scooby Snacks." These small, tasty treats have been part of the Scooby-Doo series since the very first episode.

"When do we eat?" is probably the most frequent question running through Scooby's and Shaggy's minds. Unless they're too scared to think about food! Both of them are also cowardly. Scooby is scared of the dark and of loud noises, and he is terrified of ghosts and monsters. His teeth chatter—which isn't helpful when he's trying to hide!

But Scooby can always be convinced to help his friends solve the mystery. "Will you do it for a Scooby Snack?" is a question that Scooby always answers with a "yes" and a crunch. Scooby isn't just in it for the Scooby Snacks, though. He is also very loyal. Even when he's scared, he overcomes his fear to make sure that his friends are okay. Though Scooby's not strong, he's a big guard dog with a big heart. He'll always keep a watchful eye on his friends. Until, of course, he's spooked yet again.

Veggie Power!

Casey Kasem provided the voice of Shaggy from the show's start in 1969 all the way up until 1995. Casey was a strict vegetarian who never ate meat. This became an issue when he was asked to do a

Casey Kasem

Scooby television commercial for a popular fast-food chain. Recording the commercial made him feel uncomfortable, so he quit the show. Knowing what kind of snacks Scooby and Shaggy ate was very important to Casey.

Seven years later, Casey agreed to come back to the series—but only if the character of Shaggy became a vegetarian, too. The creators agreed, and in 2002, Casey once again became the voice of Shaggy, a role he stayed with until retiring in 2009. Thanks to Casey's influence, Norville "Shaggy" Rogers was the first cartoon character to be a practicing vegetarian.

Scooby is a natural performer. He loves to dress up in costumes and disguises. Sometimes he and Shaggy will dress up to throw a monster off their trail or put on a disguise to help crack a tough case—like any good detective who needs to go undercover.

And sometimes, after a mystery's been solved, Scooby will dress up as the very monster that scared the kids in the first place—just to get a laugh! Scooby loves to have fun and play with his friends. He's also very ticklish. Shaggy and Scooby are constantly cracking each other up. It helps to take their minds off being hungry and other scary situations.

These are the things that make Scooby feel like a real pal to the people who watch his show. Children see so much of themselves in this lovable Great Dane. Who hasn't been frightened in a scary situation? Who doesn't like a snack from time to time? Scooby also reminds viewers of the importance of friendship—and the importance of helping your friends out of a jam!

CHAPTER 4
Mystery Inc.

Scooby and Shaggy are only two members of Mystery Inc.—a team of teenage detectives (and one dog) dedicated to solving the toughest mysteries. The other members of Mystery Inc. are Daphne Blake, Fred Jones, and Velma Dinkley.

Daphne, Fred, and Velma

Mystery Inc. always sticks together. They solve mysteries in spooky locations. They drive around in the "Mystery Machine," Fred's van, in search of the next mystery. And sometimes they hang out at the Malt Shop. But whatever they do, they are always a team.

Although everyone works together to solve mysteries, Fred is the leader. He always gently pushes his pals and Scooby to find the next great mystery or to search for the next big clue. Fred is smart and positive. He is also an expert at setting traps. But sometimes it's the other members of Mystery Inc. who get caught in them!

Fred likes to split up the group to look for clues. He often asks Daphne to stick with him. Daphne has a great eye for fashion. That same sharp eye is what helps her figure out what stands out in any situation—a clue! Daphne seems to stumble into the most trouble of any member of Mystery Inc. She has even been kidnapped! Daphne finds trouble so often, her nickname is "Danger-Prone Daphne."

Velma is super smart, with an incredibly fast mind. Her great brainpower helps her figure out things that others can't. Sometimes she explains the situation in a way the others don't understand. But that's okay, because she's always right. Velma may not be as danger prone as Daphne, but she does lose her glasses from time to time. Often she has to fumble around on the ground to find them because she can't see without them!

Even scaredy-cat Shaggy has his own talents. He's a talented gymnast, a ventriloquist, and an expert diver. His special skills and sense of humor make him someone the gang is always happy to have around!

Scooby-Speak

The particular way that Scooby-Doo and the gang speak has become popular with generations of fans.

Scooby is known for putting an "R" at the start of every word. This style of speech has given us new words, like "ruh-roh." People say "ruh-roh" when something bad has happened. Example: "I forgot to put the milk in the fridge last night—ruh-roh!"

The members of Mystery Inc. each have their own unique sayings. Shaggy likes to yell out "Zoinks!" right when things get the scariest. The word Daphne says whenever she's scared is "jeepers"—though people had been using "jeepers" for a long time before Daphne. Nobody knows what "jinkies" means, but Velma will say it when she's just about to solve the mystery. And "let's split up" could be considered Fred's go-to phrase.

Other cultures have made-up phrases based on Scooby-Doo: "I don't have a Scooby" is a British phrase for "I don't know!"

Shaggy and Scooby are always the first to run away (from a dangerous situation or toward a snack). But they're also the first in line to help out their friends. Once they're on the trail to solving the next mystery, there's no stopping them. And even when Scooby and Shaggy are spooked, they're usually spooked right into the next clue. They sometimes bumble into the truth, making the most of their mistakes. And always trying to stay on track!

Each member of Mystery Inc. has strengths and weaknesses. But together, they always get the job done. The gang works separately to find clues fast, coming back together at the end of their searches to compare notes. Once they know what needs to be done, they work together to set traps for the ghost, ghoul, or monster they're trying to catch. They always combine their skills to solve the mystery. For all of their differences, Mystery Inc. works like a well-oiled (but jumpy!) machine. Teamwork is their foundation.

CHAPTER 5
Scooby-Doo Takes Over TV

Children across America laughed through two seasons of *Scooby-Doo, Where Are You!* after its premiere in 1969. And Scooby-mania spread across the world! People everywhere loved the way the show always worked: Scooby and the gang investigate a spooky mystery, put together a series of clues, solve the mystery, and trap the villain (from ghosts and ghouls to demons and killer robots and everything in between). But the scary monster was always a bad guy in disguise out to steal something or to scare someone. "I would have gotten away with it, too, if it wasn't for you meddling kids!" became the tagline—a sort of slogan—used by the bad guys at the end of every show. Without fail, Mystery Inc. always caught the culprit!

But even though viewers knew how each episode would end, it didn't matter. Saturday morning became a fun time spent with Scooby and the gang. The show was always just as funny as it was spooky. The jokes were given a little boost by some really fantastic sound effects from a collection of sounds Hanna-Barbera Productions had put together for all of their cartoons.

Music played at the beginning of each episode, a catchy tune that started "Scooby-Dooby-Doo, where are you? We got some work to do now!"

This theme song became just as popular as the show! In the second season, there was even music added during the chase scenes—when Mystery Inc. was too busy running from monsters to speak.

Scooby-Doo, Where Are You! was just the beginning for Scooby. After his first television series ended, CBS created a new series: *The New Scooby-Doo Movies.* On September 9, 1972, the first episode was shown. Although it was a new series, the whole gang was still there.

There were two notable changes—first, the show was now an hour long. Second, Scooby was seeing stars! Famous guest stars from television shows and movies like *The Addams Family* and *The Three Stooges* made appearances on *The New Scooby-Doo Movies.* Famous singers Sonny & Cher and Davy Jones, and comedians Dick Van Dyke and Don Knotts were drawn as cartoon characters. Batman and Robin even

guest starred with Scooby before they had their own show, called *Super Friends*.

After two years, the twenty-four-episode run of *The New Scooby-Doo Movies* ended. *Scooby-Doo, Where Are You!* was shown in reruns. Scooby was still on television, and kids were still watching. Scooby was everywhere else, too.

By the mid-1970s, he was on all types of clothes—even on underwear! Kids could play

Scooby-Doo board games. They
could carry Scooby lunch boxes
to school. And there
were all types of
Scooby books—
coloring books,
chapter books,
and comic books.
There were even vinyl records
of Scooby-Doo stories that kids could listen to
again and again.

In 1975, Fred Silverman left his job at CBS and
went to work for another big television station,
ABC. And Fred brought Scooby along with him.
When *The Scooby-Doo Show* was added to ABC's
Saturday morning lineup in 1976, the original
idea that worked so well with *Scooby-Doo, Where
Are You!* returned—a half-hour show and no
guest stars. And Scooby had now been broadcast
on two of the "Big Three" television networks.

The Big Three

From the 1950s to the 1990s, there were only three major television channels in the United States. For three decades they were almost the only stations on television.

- National Broadcasting Company (NBC) was the first on the air in 1939.

- Columbia Broadcasting System (CBS) started in 1941.

• American Broadcasting Corporation (ABC) started in 1948.

All three began as radio networks before broadcasting television programs.

The "Big Three," as they're called, are still on the air today. But so are a large selection of other channels. As of 2016, the average American household had access to about 206 channels—although most families only watch twenty of them!

The Big Three continue to have a huge impact. One of every four hours of television viewing is still on NBC, CBS, and ABC combined. And each network is still a multibillion-dollar company!

To add a fresh element to the new show, Scooby-Dum, Scooby-Doo's cousin, came along on many of the mysteries. Scooby-Doo loved his cousin—they even had their own secret handshake—but it's clear that Scooby-Dum didn't offer much help to the gang. Perhaps that's why, as much as Scooby loved him, he eventually left the series.

Scooby-Dum

Scooby shared time before and after the broadcast of his show with other characters. Fred Silverman thought Scooby was so popular that no matter what was on before or after, kids would keep watching. He even had Hanna-Barbera Productions create all-new shows so that Scooby and the gang could appear as special guest stars.

In his first season on ABC, Scooby was part of *The Scooby-Doo/Dynomutt Hour*. And although the basic setup of the show remained the same, the gang traveled to new places. They visited some of their relatives. They headed to Washington, DC, to visit the Smithsonian Institution. They went to a football game. They even traveled to Mexico to celebrate a fiesta! But the mysteries were still just as spooky, and the bad guys were just as upset when "those meddling kids" exposed their evil plans.

From 1977 to 1978, *The Scooby-Doo Show* was part of a two-hour block of television programs: *Scooby's All Star Laff-A-Lympics*. The show started

with new episodes of *The Scooby-Doo Show* and new episodes of three other Hanna-Barbera series: *The Blue Falcon & Dynomutt*, *Captain Caveman and the Teen Angels*, and the *Laff-A-Lympics*. The *Laff-A-Lympics* was a sports-themed cartoon that featured teams of Hanna-Barbera characters—including the Scooby Doobies—competing against one another. Then the two-hour block ended with reruns of the original *Scooby-Doo, Where Are You!* shows.

For the three years that *The Scooby-Doo Show* was on the air at ABC, Saturday mornings were an epic cartoon experience!

CHAPTER 6
Puppy Power!

By the end of the 1970s, Scooby-Doo had been on the air for more than ten years. His ratings were not as high as when the original show first aired, and ABC was concerned about keeping Scooby in its Saturday morning cartoon lineup. Fred Silverman, the man who came up with the idea for Scooby, and Joe Ruby and Ken Spears, the creative guys who kept the series running, knew

it was time to create a new Scooby show. They wanted to find a new audience—and to keep Scooby fans happy at the same time. The new show would need to be fresh and a little different, so that everyone, including their bosses, would be satisfied.

The solution? A new member of the Doo family joined Scooby: his pint-size nephew, Scrappy-Doo. These two Doos couldn't be more different. Scooby was big, and Scrappy was small. Scooby was scared, and Scrappy was bold. Almost too bold! When Scooby's instinct was to run away, Scrappy would run right into danger! Luckily, Scrappy had the strength to take on whatever came his way.

Scrappy-Doo

There were other big changes when *Scooby-Doo and Scrappy-Doo* premiered on September 22, 1979. Instead of bad guys wearing masks and costumes, real ghosts, zombies, and monsters were causing all sorts of trouble! Scooby-Doo had his hands full keeping up with Scrappy on their spooky adventures, and he only had Shaggy to help. Fred, Velma, and Daphne weren't part of the new series.

But the changes worked, the ratings went up, and Scooby was once again in the spotlight thanks to his overeager nephew. Kids were soon repeating Scrappy's motto, "Puppy Power!" But some fans still missed the days when Scooby was able to solve mysteries without his nephew tagging along.

Scrappy stuck around to pester his uncle Scooby for a few more series. First, a shorter, seven-minute *Scooby and Scrappy-Doo Show* was presented with other programs (such as *Richie Rich* and *Puppy Hour*) from 1980 to 1982. This was the first Scooby-Doo television series that didn't use a laugh track.

The Laugh Track

The first radio and television comedies were performed in front of a studio audience. When they would laugh at the jokes, people listening and watching at home laughed, too!

By the early 1960s, fewer shows were performed in front of a live audience. Television producers worried that viewers, who no longer heard a laughing audience, wouldn't think the TV show was funny. So they added a recording—the sound of people laughing—to their television shows. What they added was called a "laugh track."

Though animation was always created in a studio without an audience, laugh tracks began to appear in cartoons, too. Hanna-Barbera even created its own special laugh track that it used on all of its shows in the 1970s.

Most comedy shows ended the use of laugh tracks in the 1990s.

The New Scooby and Scrappy-Doo Show premiered in 1983. The first season brought Daphne back to the cast and added another new twist: Shaggy and Daphne solved mysteries with Scooby and Scrappy while posing as writers for a teen magazine!

By the second season, the whole gang returned, and though Scrappy-Doo remained, the series was renamed *The New Scooby-Doo Mysteries.*

Then came the final TV series to feature Scrappy-Doo: *The 13 Ghosts of Scooby-Doo*. Again, only Daphne joined Shaggy, Scooby, and Scrappy on this spooky adventure.

When two ghosts spook Scooby and Shaggy into opening the "Chest of Demons," thirteen terrible spirits, the worst ghosts of all time, are released upon the world. And now—you guessed it—Shaggy, Scooby, Scrappy, and Daphne had to get all the demons back in the chest. *13 Ghosts* only lasted for one season in 1985.

No matter what changes were made to the classic Scooby story, Scooby was always top dog. After Scrappy-Doo left the show, Silverman, Ruby, and Spears decided to take the "Puppy Power" generated by Scrappy, and keep it going by making the Scooby character himself a puppy in his new series—and making the biggest change to the show so far.

In the mid-1980s, several famous TV series were "babyfied." This meant the characters were made much younger and given new shows. In many cases, they were actually so young, they were baby versions of the same characters (like *Muppet Babies*, which ran from 1984 to 1991).

In 1988, the same treatment was given to Scooby-Doo and crew. *A Pup Named Scooby-Doo* looked at what life was like for pre-teens Shaggy, Fred, Velma, and Daphne, and puppy Scooby. The show was even funnier, with new crazy expressions for each of the characters and even

sillier monsters, including the only food Scooby and Shaggy would never eat: a giant hamburger! *A Pup Named Scooby-Doo* wasn't afraid to poke fun at the Scooby-Doo universe, which made fans laugh even harder.

CHAPTER 7
Scooby Beyond Television

By the mid-1990s, reruns of Scooby's shows were still shown all over the world, but new episodes were no longer being made for television. Don Messick, the voice of Scooby, had retired. Casey Kasem, the voice of Shaggy, had quit because of the hamburger commercial.

Children still loved Scooby-Doo. After twenty-five years on television, Scooby had become part of American culture. Kids who watched the first series were now adults—and parents with their own children. They said "ruh-roh" when their own kids made mistakes.

But nobody knew if and how Scooby could continue. Would a new Scooby show work for a new generation? Could Scooby rise again to the top?

Scooby's Voice Around the World

Don Messick created the Scooby-Doo sound. He was the first actor to voice Scooby. After Don died in 1997, several actors took on the gruff but silly voice of the most popular Great Dane in America. Actor Scott Innes initially took over for Don and has voiced Scooby in everything from videos to talking Scooby toys. Neil Fanning gave the animated Scooby his voice in the movies that were shown in theaters. The most recent English-speaking voice of Scooby is Frank Welker—the actor who has voiced Fred from the beginning of the series.

From Sri Lanka to Hungary, dozens of voice actors from around the world have all put their unique spin on Scooby's sound. In most countries, different voice actors portray Scooby over time. But in others, like Japan and Brazil, a single actor has voiced Scooby for very long periods of time.

In fact, the Brazilian voice actor Orlando Drummond holds the Guinness World Record for longest-serving voice actor for one character. And that character is Scooby-Doo! Orlando has voiced Scooby in Portuguese for more than thirty-five years.

Orlando Drummond

Then the large media company Time Warner bought Hanna-Barbera Productions, the company that created Scooby-Doo. The timing was perfect for Scooby. Warner Bros. Animation (Time Warner's cartoon division) brought all the original characters back for the first time since 1984 in new full-length animated movies. Scooby had starred in five made-for-TV movies before. One of them,

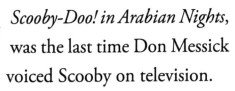

Scooby-Doo! in Arabian Nights, was the last time Don Messick voiced Scooby on television.

The new Warner Bros. feature-length movies were different—something known as a "direct-to-video" release. Before the movie was shown on television, the video, or later DVD, was first available to be purchased or rented. VCRs, the machines that played the videos, had been available in America since 1977. By the 1990s, most American homes had a VCR—and a way to play the new Scooby movies!

The first video movie, *Scooby-Doo on Zombie Island,* premiered in 1998. The Mystery Inc. gang comes together to investigate reports of the ghost of evil pirate Morgan Moonscar on a swampy island.

The mystery leads them into a deadly, supernatural adventure that includes . . . monsters! These were not just cranky old men dressed up in costumes.

Word about the new movie spread quickly. Warner Bros. spent millions of dollars promoting the film to fans. Scooby-Doo was everywhere, from Campbell's Soup labels to Lego bricks. Scooby could even be seen zooming past racing fans on a NASCAR car. Both the movie's and Scooby's popularity picked up speed!

Word of mouth spread fast. Adults who had enjoyed the original TV show rushed to watch the new movie with their children. Many of those children were watching the series for the first time—and were soon watching old episodes of *Scooby-Doo, Where Are You!* on Cartoon Network, a channel owned by the Time Warner company.

The movie earned more money than anyone had expected. Scooby-Doo was back! *Zombie Island* was followed by *Scooby-Doo! and the Witch's Ghost* in 1999, *Scooby-Doo and the Alien Invaders* in 2000, and *Scooby-Doo and the Cyber Chase* in 2001.

Scooby took his next big step—right into movie theaters! *Scooby-Doo, The Movie* had been planned since 1994. But movies are huge productions that require a big investment of both time and money to make. Now, after the success of the made-for-video films and Scooby's renewed popularity, the time was right to make the movie.

Scooby-Doo was ready for his close-up, but who could play the lovable hound on the big screen? Was any real dog up to the task? The producers of the film decided that four live-action actors would play the roles of Shaggy, Fred, Velma, and Daphne, but that Scooby-Doo would be animated. When the movie opened, a life-size animated Scooby appeared on screen with the actors.

Scooby-Doo opened in movie theaters around the world in 2002. In many ways, the movie stuck to the original story that had always worked so

well. Scooby and the gang are caught up in solving a mystery at Spooky Island amusement park. It seems that the park's owner, Mondavarious, is up to no good. *Or is he?*

Scooby solved the mystery, and the movie earned more than $275 million worldwide! Young fans watched it with their parents and grandparents. Teens and college kids wanted to see it, too. Scooby-Doo was suddenly everywhere, including back on TV, where Warner Bros. Animation developed the first new series since *A Pup Called Scooby-Doo*.

After the *Scooby-Doo* movie, Warner Bros. created a sequel, *Scooby-Doo 2: Monsters Unleashed*, in 2004. The two movies once again put lovable, goofy Scooby front and center around the world. Scooby toys, clothes, games, and more flew off the shelves, and it seemed that every child once again knew the name of this bubbly Great Dane: "Scooby-Dooby-Doo!"

CHAPTER 8
Scooby Takes Over TV ... Again!

When Scooby became an international movie star, Warner Bros. knew kids would want to see more of him. From 2002, when *Scooby-Doo* the movie burst onto the scene, Scooby could also be found every week in a new series of Scooby cartoons on television. Every few years in the 2000s and 2010s, Warner Bros. created an entirely new weekly series.

They also ran many of the old Scooby-Doo episodes. In addition, Warner Bros. released two video movies a year, always with new twists. Some of the videos showed Scooby and the gang as Lego characters. In others, Scooby solved mysteries with the help of really big guest stars—such as superstar wrestlers of the WWE, and even the

rock group KISS! There were two new live-action movies that featured new actors playing the kids of Mystery Inc., along with the same animated Scooby.

But most exciting to fans were the new weekly Scooby-Doo television series. Animation technology had changed since *A Pup Named Scooby-Doo*—from pens and paper to computers. This allowed new cartoons to be made much faster. This also allowed each new television show that featured Scooby-Doo in the 2000s and 2010s to look different from the one that had aired just a few years before.

After seventeen years, the first new series to premiere on Saturday morning television was *What's New, Scooby-Doo?* on Kids' WB in 2002. The whole Mystery Inc. gang was back. Like the original *Scooby-Doo, Where Are You!*, the monsters always turned out to be bad guys in silly outfits. The characters were made to look more modern, and they now had all sorts of new technology to help them solve the mystery. All-new sound effects and music were also featured in the show.

After three seasons, *What's New, Scooby-Doo?* was replaced by a new series on The CW's Kids' WB Saturday morning lineup, *Shaggy & Scooby-Doo Get a Clue!* In this series, Shaggy inherits money and a mansion from his uncle, Dr. Albert Shaggleford, who has gone into hiding from villains trying to steal his secret inventions. Shaggy and Scooby are stars of the show along with a newly redesigned Mystery Machine— Fred, Daphne, and Velma only make guest-starring appearances. Dr. Phineus Phibes is out to get Uncle Albert's secret inventions, and it's up to Scooby and Shaggy to stop him. The teens of Mystery Inc. were drawn to look more like the actors who played them in the new movies.

The Mystery Machine

Scooby and the gang travel in one of the coolest rides ever—the Mystery Machine. Their van has been part of Scooby-Doo shows, comics, and films from the first episode of *Scooby-Doo, Where Are You!*

The Mystery Machine has changed a bit over the years. It started as a simple van filled with ropes, ladders, and other tools for investigating and snooping. It has become a mobile headquarters for the gang, filled with high-powered computers and high-tech gadgets. It was even a news van when Daphne worked as a TV reporter.

The biggest change to the Mystery Machine was seen in *Shaggy & Scooby-Doo Get a Clue!* Shaggy added technology that could transform the van into all sorts of new villain-catching vehicles. Unfortunately, it didn't always turn into the best tool for the job—just look at the Hotdog Making Machine!

Still, Scooby and Mystery Inc. wouldn't have gotten very far without their groovy van.

In 2010, *Scooby-Doo! Mystery Incorporated* premiered on Cartoon Network. The series had a bolder, brighter animation style compared to the previous shows. It was also the first series that featured only monsters, not just scary humans, since *The 13 Ghosts of Scooby-Doo* twenty-five years before (although more "real" monsters had appeared in different versions of the videos).

Each episode of the 2010 series featured elements of many different classic horror films. It was the first time that each episode of a Scooby story led into the next, rather than being a simple, stand-alone tale. The biggest change for Scooby? He talked a lot more—and much more clearly— now. There were changes for the rest of the gang, too—they had crushes on each other!

Be Cool, Scooby-Doo!, which was first shown on Cartoon Network in 2015, is very different from *Mystery Incorporated.* In *Be Cool,* the animation became much more comical. The characters seemed a little wackier. In one episode, for instance, Daphne wears a fake beard—mainly to annoy Fred, but it ends up helping to solve the mystery.

There were many changes to Scooby and his show in the first decade of the twenty-first century, and fans always tuned in to see what the next show would look like.

CHAPTER 9
The Legacy of Scooby-Doo

Scooby-Doo is so popular, even people who haven't seen his television show know who he is. That sort of popularity is rare.

Scooby isn't just a television cartoon star. He's a movie star. And he's also a comic-book star. The comic-book series *Scooby-Doo! Where Are You?* is the longest-running comic that's not about

a superhero from DC Comics! Scooby-Doo has also been a Marvel comic. And he's been featured in thousands of other comics as well.

Like the TV series, new comic-book series change the Scooby stories to keep them fresh. Some comic books create completely different worlds for Scooby. The gang must save the entire world from monsters by using new weapons and some pretty crazy technology in *Scooby Apocalypse.*

In this 2016 comic, Scooby can talk because of a microchip implanted in his brain—and he even wears "emoji-goggles" to show people how he feels.

Scooby has been the star of eleven major video games, some that were based on his TV show, and some that told their own story—like *Scooby Doo! Who's Watching Who?* His first video game, *Scooby-Doo*, boasted to be the "first ever computer cartoon" in 1986.

Scooby has been featured in three amusement rides, including "Scooby's Ghoster Coaster," which opened in 1998 at Kings Island in Ohio. The play *Scooby-Doo in Stagefright* was performed around the world in the 2000s. And Scooby has even entered monster-truck competitions! The Scooby-Doo truck was so popular when it competed in Monster Jam races and stunts in

2013 that by 2016, there were four trucks—all driven by female drivers.

So, Scooby has been almost everywhere and done almost everything!

But television made Scooby the superstar he is today.

In 1989 and 1990, *A Pup Named Scooby-Doo* was nominated for a Daytime Emmy Award for Outstanding Children's Animated Program. In 2003, voice actor Mindy Cohn (who played Velma) was also nominated for a Daytime Emmy Award. In 2004, the Scooby-Doo series held the Guinness World Record for most episodes of any cartoon produced. In 2013, Scooby-Doo was ranked number five in *TV Guide Magazine*'s "60 Greatest Cartoons of All Time." And in 2016, voice actor Frank Welker was honored with a Lifetime Achievement Award from the Daytime Emmys, in part because of his work voicing both Fred and Scooby!

Mindy Cohn

Daytime Emmy Awards

Since 1949, the Emmy Awards have been the top honor for television programs.

The honors are awarded by the Television Academy, a group made up of all types of creative people who make television shows: from actors and directors to writers and producers and more. The Academy figures out who to nominate and then votes for their favorites in a number of different categories.

In 1972, the Daytime Emmy Awards, honoring daytime television, were created. The top award for cartoons is the Award for Outstanding Children's Animated Program, which has been given out since 1985. Some past winners include *Arthur*, *Muppet Babies*, and *Rugrats*.

But more important than awards and honors, Scooby taught generations of children that if they were true to themselves, no matter how scared or quirky or silly, they could save the day.

Mystery Inc. is a group of friends first, and a mystery-solving team second. Sometimes Velma was annoyed with Daphne ("Danger-Prone

Daphne did it again!"). Sometimes Scooby and Shaggy spent too much time stealing each other's food and not enough time searching for clues. Fred's traps only worked half the time. Velma kept losing her glasses. It was okay to be scared. They were friends to the end, always there to have each other's back.

In real life, groups of good friends sometimes compare themselves to the gang, pointing out who's who. Are you a Fred (the leader)? Or are you a Velma (the smart one)? Scooby's brand of friendship has found its way into other television shows as well. Characters in the famous television series *Buffy the Vampire Slayer* refer to themselves as "The Scooby Gang."

Most importantly, Scooby taught us that sometimes the scariest things aren't monsters, zombies, or ghosts, but regular people who aren't very nice. And it's up to good friends working together to reveal the truth.

What made Scooby-Doo so popular for so long is that he was a simple character who we all felt like we knew. Viewers enjoyed the chases, the thrills, and the scary stories as much as the funny antics of this crazy canine. As Casey Kasem, the original voice of Shaggy, said, "Kids are a lot like Scooby." Children—and adults—all see a little bit of themselves in Scooby-Doo.

CHAPTER 10
What's Next for Scooby-Doo?

Scooby-Doo is one of the most recognizable cartoon characters around the world. He's been on television for almost fifty years—that's half a century! He's starred in blockbuster movies. And he's been in countless videos, comic books, and video games.

What's next for Scooby? It seems like that question has been asked since the premiere of *Scooby-Doo, Where Are You!* The story from that original show will continue to be told in ways that will make Scooby even more popular, for generations to come. Scooby-Doo will continue on TV with a new series, *Scooby-Doo and Guess Who?* Scooby will continue to star in made-for-video movies as well. Wherever new technologies bring Scooby, fans are sure to follow. Scooby has more than twenty-five million likes on Facebook! He's on Pinterest, Instagram, and Snapchat, too. Dozens of Scooby-Doo apps—from games to learning tools for children—are enjoyed on mobile devices.